BIG CABIN

BIG CABIN
RON PADGETT

COFFEE HOUSE PRESS

Minneapolis

2019

Coffee House Press books are available to the trade through our primary distributor, Consortium Book Sales & Distribution, cbsd.com or (800) 283-3572. For personal orders, catalogs, or other information, write to info@coffeehousepress.org.

Coffee House Press is a nonprofit literary publishing house. Support from private foundations, corporate giving programs, government programs, and generous individuals helps make the publication of our books possible. We gratefully acknowledge their support in detail in the back of this book.

LIBRARY OF CONGRESS CATALOGING-IN-PUBLICATION DATA

Names: Padgett, Ron, 1942– author.
Title: Big cabin / Ron Padgett.
Description: Minneapolis : Coffee House Press, 2019. | Includes
    bibliographical references and index.
Identifiers: LCCN 2018049838 (print) | LCCN 2018059280 (ebook) |
    ISBN 9781566895576 (ebook) | ISBN 9781566895491 (trade paper :
    alk. paper)
Subjects: LCSH: American poetry—21st century.
Classification: LCC PS3566.A32 (ebook) | LCC PS3566.A32 A6 2019
    (print) | DDC 813/.54—dc23
LC record available at https://lccn.loc.gov/2018049838

ACKNOWLEDGMENTS

Some of the poems in this book appeared in a series of limited-edition artists' books, under the title *From a Cabin in the Woods*, published in France by Collectif Générations, directed by Gervais Jassaud. "Wristwatch" was featured in the Academy of American Poets's online Poem-a-Day series. Tom Clark included "On Fire" in his blog, *Beyond the Pale.* "And Truly" came out in *New World Writing* and *Chasm Journal,* both online magazines. "In the Winter of 1969–70" was published in *Aphros.* "Harold Clough" was published in *The Volta.* "Haiku" was made into a broadside for the Adamant, VT, Poem City 2018 event. "Sandwich" was printed in the *Ocean State Review.* Many thanks to the editors of these publications.

PRINTED IN THE UNITED STATES OF AMERICA

26 25 24 23 22 21 20 19   1 2 3 4 5 6 7 8

Contents

1.

2.

3.

BIG CABIN

For Dick Gallup

1

Big Cabin

I like it here in this cabin.
I like looking out the window
at the pond and the trees beyond
and with quiet inside.
Sixty years ago I was a boy
with a baseball glove in Oklahoma,
looking down at it and knowing
I would give it away
and not buy a new one.

The Up Side

The pines are
stately

still

reflecting
upon themselves

without knowing it

in eternity

upside down.

And Truly

We use italics
to put electricity into words.
Then we plug lamps
into the words.
That's how we light our homes.
Really.

Chickadee

The chickadees went away
a few months ago
delightful little things

Now they're back
chattering away

Wait for me
I'm the biggest chickadee
in the world

Glump glump

Clocked

I'm going to look at my watch
though I don't really care what time it is.
Just slightly curious.
It's funny when you see
it's much earlier or later
than you thought,
but even funnier when it's *exactly*
the time you thought.

But at my back etc.
Etc. being
"Desarts of vast Eternity."

I give up.
It's eleven eleven.

What ever happens
at eleven eleven?
Vast eternity!

Thin

My skin has grown
thinner, as thin
as the paper
on which I write.
Sometimes
I accidentally cut myself
and don't even know it:
a thin line of blood is there.
It's hard to talk to.

People

People are so
fucking nutty
it's amazing
that we get through
the day
without one of them
undoing the parts
of his body
and then putting them
back together
in the wrong places
right in front of us.

Sandwich

I'm in a cabin
about 300 yards
from my house
in the woods
on a cold, damp day,
sky overcast bright gray.
At home
in the fridge
is sliced ham
I will put
between two slices of bread
with mustard
and raise the ensemble
to my mouth
and go chomp,
a chomp
300 yards away.

Hope

Is there any hope for you
or anyone else?
Sure there is,
but hope for what?

Hope isn't *for* anything.
It's just a big bunch of feeling.

Harold Clough

In 1895 or thereabouts
Harold Clough was born
in East Calais, Vermont.
I knew him for the last oh
twenty-five years of his life,
and deep into that time
I thought to talk with him
with a tape recorder running.

I never did.
You'll never hear his voice
saying anything.
What a dope I am.

When he started driving a car
there was no such thing
as a driver's license.

He was under five feet tall,
with huge hands and feet,
and his hair stuck out
from beneath his dirty baseball cap
like quills on a porcupine.

It didn't bother him
to hold live wires
and he could find water
with a stick or coat hanger,
it didn't matter which.

The skin on his hands was so tough
he could just reach in
and take a pie out of the oven.

He showed me how to hold a nail
and at the same time
to drive it with a hammer—
using only one hand.

Around eighty he discovered *Playboy,*
amazed that he could see those girls
all totally naked and glowing, right there.

He once mailed a donut to my dog.

He knew how to lift a barn
all by himself.

One day I got a call from a friend
who said, "Old Harold just died.
In the hospital. Heart attack."

An hour later
the friend called back:
"Harold ain't dead.
He come back to life."
Not only that, when the nurse returned
he was sitting up and smiling.

A few years later he really did die,
of a fire, in the house
he was born in.

I once asked him for his mailing address.
"You can put Harold Clough,
East Calais, Vermont.
Or Harold Clough, Adamant.
Or North Montpelier.
Woodbury. Or Calais.
Don't matter none. It'll get to me."

In the Winter of 1969–70

In the winter of 1969–70
I went out to an old shed
behind Fairfield Porter's house
and fired up the coal stove,
cleared a spot on a workbench,
sat down and started translating
the poetry of Blaise Cendrars.
Sometimes the room got so hot
I'd open the door wide open
and outside snow was falling.
It was one of the happiest times of my life.

Life without You

I leap from the title to this first line as if over a stream
and find myself on the other side, safe
but for how long there is no way of knowing.
The wind dances the trees lightly
and the leaves rustle as if they are happy to be moving
instead of just hanging there all day.
I think I will like it here, but I will
have to forget about a great many things,
in fact almost everything, including you
and thus myself. A piano note
appears in the air.

It has leaped as if over nothingness
to be here with you, and soon
other notes appear, lined up and going up
and down in one long wave that says hello
to no one in particular, except you
are particular, a dust mote,
an idea one almost has.

What's the matter with matter?
Something has to be wrong with it, no?
Or is something wrong with you? Oh
plenty. The mole, the squirrel, the flying fish
didn't ask to be matter, they don't ask anything;
who would answer them? Not I,
said the little red dot. And thus the dress
your mother wore in 1948.

The year 1948 leaps out of itself
and lands on your doorstep,
a writhing mass of strings and bubbles,

and when you open the door and peer out
there is only a drawing of the street where you currently live
in black and white. Across the ocean
the colors are vibrating,
as if preparing to come your way,
and there is no way of stopping them,
for they want to wrap their mysticism
around you and carry you off in their traveling circus.
They need a clown.

Paul Eluard

Paul Eluard said,
"There is another world
but it's in this one"
or something to that effect.
I would say,
"Everything is odd enough
as it is"
or something to that effect.
My handwriting, for example,
and my hand writing.
Hand, say hello to Paul Eluard.

Lunch Jr.

Saved again by lunch!
At school at work at home
millions of people
are saved by lunch!
I put the words
right into my mouth.

It's Good

It's good to have a heater
you can hold your hands in front of
to get them warm enough to hold a pen
to write "It's good to have a heater,"
and to feel the warmth
spreading into your knees
and down your shins
though you can't do much with them
in a sitting position.
They're just down there
being shins.

Ticking and Tocking

When people say
"Time is running out"
I see an alarm clock
with a bell on top
and with arms and legs
dashing out the door
of a room in which
time has stopped
reminding the human race
that *we* are running out.

I carry this idea
to a corner of the room
and set it down
gently.
I don't want
to wake it up.
Then I tiptoe away.

Sweeping Away

What I want to do
is to forget everything
I ever knew about poetry
and sweep the pine needles
off the cabin roof
and watch them fly away
into this October afternoon.

The pen is mightier than the sword
but today the broom
is mightier than the pen.

Poem

You're here—
and if you relax
for a moment
your back
and other parts
will arrive
and you can be
together,
with yourself,
a little happiness.

On Fire

The afternoon light across the pond
is doing a good job today, the sky
a gray smudge with a trace of puffery
but the trees stand out in perfect clarity
and here I am, and if I weren't
I wouldn't know the difference,
just as, say, Shelley wouldn't.
"O sky and song entwinèd in a wild embrace
and hid asleep inside the human race,"
he might have said.
It's good to think of Shelley
as a person and not
the great Romantic poet
who died at thirty tragically,
Percy a young man gifted and serious
with a big heart and an open mind
who wrote some mediocre poems
and a few truly great ones.
Every night I read a few and try
to see him writing them, but
all I get is a dim view of the back
of a man at a table in a chilly room in Italy,
his arm moving slightly,
and in the flickering candlelight a woman
with a sleeping baby in her arms.
From time to time the baby says "Umph"
and another sheet of paper flutters down
with flowing, glistening words in black.
Shelley is on fire tonight.

The Hook

All it takes is a hook
even a small one
of any color
and you're in. Today
it's gray that grabs you
and won't let go
and you don't want it to.
It's a tree.

The Porcupine

If you've ever come face-to-face
with a porcupine
you know how beast-like they look,
but to the porcupine
you are of very little interest,
like a stone on the ground,
though unlike a stone you wave
your arms and shout "Hey!"
The porcupine swivels his head
and waddles a few feet away.
He isn't very funny.

Songs of the Skeleton

1.

How interesting it would be
if one could suddenly dart ahead
of one's body and turn around
and see it standing there, dumbfounded!
But to leave it there like that
would be sad.

2.

I've known people who thought
they were someone else
and then came back
to being themselves,
though sometimes they seemed
uncertain, as if that other person
were about to sneak up behind them
and go *Boo!*

3.

When I was a child
I knew skeletons
were *supposed* to be scary.

4.

When you see a real skeleton
you know that one day
those bones were walking around
inside someone who was whistling
and feeling good about being alive
and not thinking
about some day becoming a skeleton.

5.

Most skeletons would be lying
if they said,
"I am the skeleton of Shakespeare."

6.

Jesus was almost a skeleton,
which is one reason he came for dinner—
or, as they called it, The Last Supper.
It's better than coming for The Last Lunch,
though if you're really hungry
you just eat anytime, and your body
loves you for it,
and you're in a kind of heaven.

Plume

A path wends its way
through the woods
to a whitewashed cottage
with thatched roof, a plume
of smoke on top.
Is the cottage on fire?
No, it is not.
I won't let it be.
I will open its door
and find you there again,
my plume, my smoke.

Wristwatch

I've just written six
or seven short poems
in about half an hour,
in a cabin
on a pond
with raindrops.
Maybe I should
just sit here
for a while, let
some time pass
so my wife will think
I've been working hard.

See that?
Some time just went past
but so quietly
you might have missed it.
It morphed
into the sky.
Look, another one!
It came out
of my wristwatch
and morphed away.

I Give Up

I give up
for today
but I'll be back
tomorrow
with my pen
and paper and identity
that keeps an eye on things.

2

Completion

I am writing this in a school notebook whose puzzling name, printed on the front cover in large type, is *Completion,* with a sort of subtitle: "Take your fun where you can find it." The notebook was made in Japan, which perhaps offers some explanation of why this peculiar title and subtitle have been joined in such an unlikely place.

I am in a place that is neither likely nor unlikely: a cabin on a pond in rural Vermont. I have come here to write in this notebook—for reasons that are even more mysterious than the notebook's title. I can say with certainty, though, that I am sitting at a small, cheaply made table with fold-down aluminum legs, which an artist friend of mine bought thirty-five years ago, and if I part the curtains in front of me I will see the same view as I did around forty-five years ago when I sat in this very cabin writing poetry, two poems in particular ("Radio" and "Arrive by Pullman"). The pond made an appearance in the latter when rain started to fall. It rained earlier this morning as well, but now the sky is just an overcast gray. But weather is not what I had in mind when I thought of coming here to write in this notebook. I was thinking about . . . or rather I had an *impulse* to write about aloneness.

That word struck me as just right, but odd. Shouldn't one say *solitude?* No, solitude is something else. In solitude you have no one around you. With aloneness you can have others around you or not. Solitude is usually good. Aloneness is usually not, at least in the way I'm thinking of it.

To be honest, my thoughts on the subject are vague. The one thing I do understand clearly is that being an only child has had such an all-encompassing effect on me that for most of my life I was unable to perceive that effect. Growing up, all I knew was that I was glad I didn't have to share a room with anyone. My friends and classmates had brothers and sisters who were mostly annoying, to hear them tell of it. But as I have grown older, the impact of being an only child has revealed itself more deeply, and what I thought of as a privileged status has begun to feel like a deprivation.

Fortunately, I have a wife, a son, a daughter-in-law, two grandchildren, and a sister-in-law, as well as a number of friends, some for more than half a century. This takes the edge off my aloneness—the soothing effect of being with people I would give my life for. This deep bonding (let's call it that, for want of a better word) . . .

I forgot what I was going to say! I *do* know that I was preparing myself to leap into the image of a man holding his head in his hands, not from fatigue or dismay or grief, but simply as a way of having the physical sensation of encircling his inner self, of locating it in the material world, for I believe, simplistically perhaps, that my self is centered in my head, or at least spends the great majority of its time there. By *self* I mean the conscious self, the one you can talk with, the one whose thoughts are in the words you think and are aware of thinking, and even in the semiconscious self, the one of half-sleep and intuition, of unexpected conceptual jumps and seemingly bizarre associations. It's the self that appears on waking and fades out in sleep. In short, it's the person you have to live with all day. You might like this person or you might not—which of course is very important for your everyday life—but either way you are stuck with being who you think you are, and though the identity of that person can evolve over time, the fact of its being there does not change, until you die. And after that . . .

■ ■ ■

I have drawn aside the curtains and taken a glance at the pond. Its surface is absolutely still. In fact everything outside is immobile—trees, sky, air. The only things moving are my arm, hand, and pen, though from time to time I shift in my chair and take a swig from a small bottle of water.

What if suddenly I had no wife, no family at all? Such things have happened to people—I'm thinking of the Holocaust—and continue to happen—the Middle East. Or Middle America. Suddenly they're gone. How do you manage to go on living? Clearly you could not be your "old" self anymore. But where do survivors find the strength to endure such violent revisions of reality? I can't imagine being able to. I do not have the physical stamina, nor do I have the emotional strength, the strong self as an independent entity capable of not only surviving but also of taking some pleasure in life. I depend on those close to me, more than they know. Yes, yes, I'm a writer who is convinced that he is a writer, that it matters, and that the time I devote to it and not to my family is justifiable, but when I peel away my identity as a writer, a husband, a father, and so on, right down to the isolated creature that I fundamentally am, I turn away from that creature, unable to look into its sad, bewildered eyes that seem to be asking—aha!—the same eternal questions that arise in a sensitive adolescent: Why am I cursed with consciousness? Am I the result of a freak accident in the universe? Is the universe itself a freak accident? And why do I have a consciousness that presses these questions on me? Why can't I be more like an ant, dutifully shuttling to and fro as part of a society in which the idea of anxiety does not exist? In fact no idea exists! Surely the universe would go on without ideas in it.

In my first year of college I read *The Origins and History of Consciousness* by Erich Neumann. As I recall, he offered a psychological interpretation of the story of the Garden of Eden: the expulsion of Adam and Eve symbolized the birth of higher consciousness, when humans separated themselves out from animals. Thus the triumph, however tenuous, of the conscious over the unconscious entailed a loss as well, the loss of innocence, that is, the loss of being an animal unaware of its own mortality, but also the loss of the bond with the other animals of the earth. Humanity had taken the first step toward isolating itself, and it would seem that we have taken many more steps in that direction, to the point that now we are isolating ourselves from one another. The final step would be to isolate ourselves from ourselves, in effect erasing our humanity. If you want to see that in a positive light, imagine it as a return to the Garden of Eden. Except that the Garden itself would be gone, too.

■ ■ ■

Give a man pen and paper and he will obliterate the Garden of Eden!

I look out the window. Small ripples on the pond, fog in the treetops—was it there before? The day is ahead of me: things to do, things to think about doing, and whatever happens to come up. I will be normal, the way the person I am known to be is normal. I am by no means saying that this is a bad thing. After all, one cannot live entirely in an existential quandary. We need breakfast, too. And in the end who is to say that breakfast is less important than quandariness, or even that the two aren't fundamentally the same thing in different forms? That is, you do what you do.

■ ■ ■

Aside from a bit of amateur psychology, I have never been able to understand other people. That is, to grasp what drives them. Perhaps no one does, but what surprised me was how long it took me to realize that my knowledge of other people, even those I called my best friends, was superficial. Perhaps this is one of the reasons I have gotten along with them so well, another reason being our deep affinities, despite our differences. Little did I suspect that as they died, one by one, they would take a little part of me with them, just as I kept part of them. Or so I believe. Perhaps this is simply a way of making their absence less . . . I was about to say *painful,* but *empty* is a better word for it. Outside the window the pond is only a few feet away, and I can't help but see Joe on it again, floating around in the afternoon sun, his eyes closed as he goes into a deeper relaxation, the little floatation mattress under him slowly rotating and drifting. And suddenly they come back—Anne Kepler, Ted, and George, my mother and father, my grandparents—and I feel as if it is my fate to represent them, which I do, automatically, by being alive.

■ ■ ■

And so we have the voice in our head, the one we think of as ours, the one we have listened to and even replied to since early childhood, when words became things and not just meaningless sounds. ("I can pick up that word and move it over there!") And so, the dialogue that lasts a lifetime, the dialogue that sustains us no matter how tedious or repetitious it becomes.

Can you have a thought that is *completely* unlike any you've ever had? I don't think I can. The words for it seem to be locked out of my head, where my consciousness is dashing around looking for something it can't find—and doesn't even know what it is. The day goes by, and late in the evening the mind assumes it has done its best and turns part of itself off for a while, leaving the other part to do whatever it does. I used to put great stock in that other part—the dream life—and I suppose I still do, but now the paradigm of conscious versus unconscious seems utterly simplistic. There is something beyond my concept of my own mind, beyond my sense of my self, but I do not know what it is.

A dragonfly hovered over the water's surface for a moment, then sped on, as if with an absolute sense of purpose.

The new pine boards in this cabin smell good.

■ ■ ■

If I sit and wait long enough, something will come to me. That's a little like saying that if you stand long enough on a mountaintop during an electrical storm you will eventually be struck by lightning. And the light bulb above your head will explode!

■ ■ ■

My penchant for comic book imagery comes partly from having immersed myself in comic books as a child, alone in my room but not really alone, since I was with my friends Daffy Duck, Little Lulu, Plastic Man, Sad Sack, and a host of others, all of whom lived in a world in which order prevailed and the colors were bright. Most other children were unpredictable, their eating habits strange, their clothes unmatched. Actually, all my friends were boys.

Girls were objects of attraction, glowing with vague, romantic auras. Aside from a tomboy cousin, I didn't have a girl as a friend until I was in high school, and even she had been an object of attraction. Finally accepting that she was not going to return my full affection, I made a big adjustment that allowed her to be my friend, while all the time trying to figure out who she really was and what she wanted from life (and from me). I never succeeded in doing that, and when she died, at the age of twenty-three . . . I still see her as she was and for a moment I yearn to go inside her mind, and then I tell myself to stop wanting the impossible. Still, the urge does not go away, the urge to understand my dead friends and to go back and rescue them from the fate that took their lives. A classic case of regret, survivor guilt, or something worse! I should know better, and I do, but I don't. Why do I subject myself to such yearning? Why can't I be contented with looking out this window at the inverted reflection of tall pines and spruces, quavering on the water, the light blue-gray sky below them?

When written down, such a "poetic" image is at first pleasing, then mainly distracting, which makes me dislike it, though I like it out there on the pond, the "real" pond.

■ ■ ■

Over the past several years I have been compiling a list of expressions that were common in my childhood but are very rarely heard these days, if at all. This morning I remembered another one, though not a particularly good example: *Bats in the belfry*. As a child I knew what it meant even before I learned what a belfry was.

It turns out that what I really miss are not the expressions themselves, but the contexts in which I heard them. I miss words like *buckager,* but what I miss even more is hearing my grandmother say it, and the living room in her home, with my grandpa tilted back a little in his recliner on a Saturday afternoon, stockinged feet elevated, and grandma in the doorway to the adjoining dining room, through which she came from the kitchen to join momentarily in the conversation, with Ernest Tubb or Bob Wills on the big brown console radio across the room, near the front door.

I still listen to the radio and I still like old-time country music, and sometimes when I pass by a mirror I catch a fleeting aspect of my grandfather's face, so that in a sense all these things have not utterly vanished. But I am crazy (or juvenile) enough to want my real grandpa to still be there in his recliner, everything exactly the same for all eternity. In fact I want every moment of my life to still be there, the same, for eternity.

Perhaps an unconscious dependency on this yearning has kept me from making a greater effort to understand the people I have felt close to. What did my grandfather think about when he was alone? How did he feel about himself? Men of his time and class left very few records of such things. Even the diaries of rural and working-class people, kept, I think, mostly by women, often are made up of short, factual notations, such as "Cold and cloudy today. Helen visited."

What's that big ripple in the pond? Aha! The brown head of a beaver, cruising around, looking for what? Maybe it's a muskrat—I don't have my distance glasses. I look back up from the page. The head has disappeared. No, now it's back, and I can see more of the body, a length of twelve to eighteen inches along the spine. It seems to be holding something white in its teeth, unless the white *is* its teeth. Now another critter comes gliding across the pond—a small duck that goes over to some water lilies and seems to be feeding on something there. Seeing animals like this always strikes me as a privilege—a reaction that rural people would find amusing, the way I stifled a laugh when a working-class rural friend of mine in his late seventies, visiting New York City for the first time and looking down from the top of the Empire State Building at the streets below, kept exclaiming, "Look at all those yellow taxicabs!"

■ ■ ■

Who was it that used to say, "I got tired of hearing myself think"? (There must be people who would say the opposite: "I am very pleased to hear myself think.") Being unable to get a song out of one's head is aggravating, an extreme version of hearing oneself think in the same way too often. Maybe that's part of my problem. Do you remember when someone would say to another person who was repeating himself or herself, "Hey, the needle's stuck"? If you don't know what a record player is, with the needle in its tone arm, then that expression will mean nothing to you. But then you probably use expressions that mean nothing to me. That's the way the world is. However, we *can* make an effort to understand each other, even though we hardly understand ourselves. It is not given to us to understand everything, being swept along in the flow of life in which a million things are happening in and around us at every moment, and now sunlight falls across this page, as if making a cryptic comment on what I just wrote, like the fly that landed in the words of the poem "À la Santé" that Apollinaire was writing in jail. A few years later he was shuddering in the horrendous trenches in Champagne, bullets and artillery shells whizzing and exploding, poison gas drifting toward him, rotting corpses left and right. And here I sit, in a little cabin on a placid four-acre pond surrounded by pine trees, sunlight slanting through the window to my right, the only sound that of my pen scribbling away. What right do I have to bemoan my fate? The right that a spoiled only child assumes all too easily, virtually as a birthright.

■ ■ ■

I took a peek at an earlier part of this writing: "To be honest, my thoughts on the subject are vague." That sounds exactly like something I wrote fifty-seven years ago, at the age of fourteen. Perhaps I should get up from this chair and dust the windowsills. Or accept the fact that a fourteen-year-old boy occupies too large a space in my psyche.

He desperately wanted to be loved by a girl, a girl he was in love with, but it was not to be. A year or so later there was another girl, only this time I was not perplexed by her, I was fascinated by what I saw as the impenetrable depths of her soul. Again, my love was unrequited, but she did give me her companionship, and she said something that jolted me: "Why do you go by the name of Ronnie? You're not a kid anymore.

Ron sounds much more mature." From that moment on I was Ron. Years later I considered using my legal name, Ronald, but it sounded too formal for the person I am, and I'm still not happy that I was named after the film star who went on to become president. For a moment just now I tried to imagine what it was like to be Ronald Reagan, but the vision of it was so disturbing that I stopped myself.

I've never wanted to be anyone else, but being satisfied with one's own identity leads easily to a complacency about it, and though by my age it's better to accept than to reject oneself, that doesn't mean one should not be open to change. Staying open isn't easy, but it seems like an optimistic thing to do, and optimism is something we could all use more of.

■ ■ ■

I should be open to the idea that it is not a tragedy that writing in this notebook has brought me no closer to discovering what it was I might have been looking for, particularly since there is no way of knowing what it might have been. I came here not to find a pond, but in an odd way I *did* find one, one that I am happier than ever to be with. I found the new-sawn pine smell of the cabin walls. I found quiet. And I found a kind of release, however temporary, from the urge to understand. Perhaps now I can dust these windowsills without feeling that it's an evasion from doing something more meaningful. Perhaps I can now let the raindrops, which have started to fall into the pond, just be raindrops.

3

Rock around the Table

When I walked across the floor
the table wobbled a little
and the pen on it wobbled too,
making a rock-rock-rock sound
as if telling me
to either stop walking
or start writing.
I've done both—this
poem proves it.
Actually this poem proves nothing.
Fortunately I don't *have* to prove anything.
I can move around in the world
and just . . . move around.
Until a pen goes rock-rock-rock.

The Wanderer

I forgot to bring my watch.
Bright gray morning sky, no hint
of the sun.
I left the house around 9
and I've been here for . . .
an hour? Less,
I think.
        I have
a pond, a forest, a gray sky,
and a mind that wanders
from moment to moment.

Almost Statue

Am I going to end up liking myself?
It could go either way.
But is it important,
liking oneself? It helps

but it involves a lot of *self.*
What would I be
without my self?
Maybe a statue.
But what's the point of being a statue?

Maybe I could be *part* me, part statue.
Is that possible?
Yes, for a psycho or a saint.

Timex Blur

I was going to complain
about how irritating it is
to have to change one's clock
twice a year and not
understand why, but sunlight
just came down and hit
the pond and my brain
at the same time.

Things to Do

Today: collect
trash, put
in truck, take
to dump, sweep
out truck bed,
feel love
for truck,
then do other things
I'm supposed to do
but can't, fortunately,
remember now.
What I remember now
is from a moment ago,
seeing my father appear
in my mind's eye,
then not.

Down Under

People are wont to repeat the old advice
"Live every day
as if it were the last day of your life."
The last day of my life? What?
I'd be frantic, jumping
around like a kangaroo
in boxing gloves
and punching the air,
trying to fight off
whatever.
What people mean is
"Be fully engaged with life."
Like a kangaroo without boxing gloves.

Shanghai Cutout

Charlie Chaplin is on the wall
up near the ceiling,
a paper cutout of him
about ten inches tall
and hinged at the joints,
in his Little Tramp costume,
held up there by a nail
through a hole in his hat.

I stayed at the Astor House hotel
in Shanghai
as he once did,
though of course
it was a different Shanghai,
and I was a different cutout.

Haiku

First, calm down.
Next, stay that way
for the rest of your life.

Sideways Guy

I happened to catch
a glimpse of myself
in an old mirror,
cruddy and mottled
(the mirror, not me):
late medieval old guy
turned slightly and stopped,
black stocking cap sticking up
and eyes not exactly dead
but lacking the quickness of youth,
fixed on you as if
on someone you don't care about
one way or the other.

Infusion

It feels cold in this room
until I go outside.
Is that a metaphor
waiting for its meaning?
Probably.
Isn't everything waiting for its meaning?
Go ahead,
infuse everything with meaning.
See how far it'll get you.

People vs. Leaves

Clever and powerful people
have taken control over my life
but for some reason
I don't care,
for I have that pile of leaves
over there.
Those people are wasting their lives
day after day.

For a moment I feel sorry for them
but then I look at the leaves
and don't care
what happens to humanity.

But if humanity disappears
who will read this poem?
Fuck.

Inside Happiness

Let's get inside a song
and live there,
happy in its refrain,
happy to be in it
again and again,
always the same.

It's Quite Something

It's quite something
how those ducks
out there on the pond
with fog drifting over them
don't seem to be cold
in the icy water—
my fingers cold
as the pen slides along
and veers around a metaphor.
Where'd the ducks go?

More about Whitehead

Was it Whitehead
who said that
there is no distinct line
between one's body
and the air around it,
that along the boundary
atoms are constantly
being exchanged?
I knew one of his students,
Anne Porter.
Maybe some of his atoms
stuck to her
and decades later
got transferred to me.
What a charming thought!
(And idiotic.)

Auditorium

No telephone, no computer,
no people, no cars, no TV
or radio, not even a refrigerator
to shudder and clunk off,
just the sound of water
flat with a few ripples—
that is, no sound of water.
For a moment
I hear its no-soundness
and then
a slow wave of chuckling,
an auditorium of children
all hearing the same joke
in their heads. Ah!
A happy pond!

A New Leaf

It all stems
from the fact
that I am a gay blade
who wants to turn over
a new leaf
because the grass
is always greener
on the other side
of everything.
Ah! there's
a new leaf
created out
of nothing,
hanging in the air
in front of my face
that suddenly turns
inside out
with joy.

OK

I'll bet that not one
in ten thousand people
knows where the expression OK
came from
and yet all over the world
even people who don't speak English
say it every day.
That's how it works,
"it" being life.
We don't understand much of anything
but it's OK!
(I guess.)

Any Future

Like a creature from the future,
glowing orange and rising
from a pond but
then frozen in place above it,
the reflection in the windowpane
of the elements of the electric heater
seem to be on the verge
of telling me something
I could never have imagined,
such as "I am all
that's left of you."
Who would want to be a heating element
in the future? Who really
wants the future?

My Eye

To disagree with someone
we used to say
"My eye!"
How did I
as a child
know that this
had nothing to do
with an eye?

"My eye!"
was a sharp stick
I could wave defiantly—
at nobody, really,
because at heart
I was a nice kid.

Long Distance

Drops of water drop
from the pine branch
over the pond
and for each drop a widening ring
is overlapping other rings
in the sky,
rings and rings and rings
up there in total silence.

To Yu Jian

Though we speak different languages
we seem to understand each other.
All it takes is a look in the eye,
a slight smile,
a gesture, and
we know.
We know how to get along well
because we respect each other
and we assume a lot.
Someday I'd like to talk with you
for hours and hours,
to see what would happen.
You are a completely interesting person.

The 19s

The sun rises and there's more.
I can say I've lived
until Tuesday, October 27,
in the year 2015,
a number that still sounds odd.
How can a year be
2015?
I prefer the numbers of the twentieth century.
They all sound good.

Topknot and All

Reeds at the pond's edge
bending and waving in the wind,
a long running row of them
like in a black-and-white Japanese film,
and here comes a sword
and two fierce eyes in the head of a man
who flies up and vanishes into the air.

A Big *Almost*

I can almost imagine
what it was like
to be my mother,
with emphasis on *almost*.
Her feelings about being
in this, the only world,
rise up in me
and are turned away
by my personality.
It wants to be itself,
not someone else,
though that someone else
is only a few molecules away.

The Cloud

I should read *The Cloud of Unknowing* again.
It's been fifty years.
I can't remember what it said,
so maybe I don't have to read it again.
Maybe I'm the Cloud!
A wisp of it.

The Ripple Effect

Joe said
"If you paint a tree
that looks exactly like a tree,
no one will believe you."
Likewise anything,
like the million ripples
rippling into each other's glitter:
If I tell someone
about those ripples they'll think
"Uh oh" and look away.
I'm going to anyway.

Ducks

It makes me sad to think
I'm petty—where'd
those ducks go? Off
to the left, I think,
then south, for sure.
I'm starting to get nervous
about following them.
I should leave them alone.
I should leave myself alone.

Chinese Twins

When I was in China
I had the sudden desire
to be in a cabin in Vermont
remembering the moment
when I felt that way

and now I'm here
in the cabin
but without a desire to be in China,
not at this moment, anyway.
I don't need that desire:
the two moments were just connected
like Siamese twins
who have just learned how to talk to each other.

The Triumph of Beavers

Is there any evidence
that a surrealist
ever saw a beaver?
I know it's a trivial question
but I'm wondering.
I imagine the face of a surrealist
and the face of a beaver
as they suddenly see each other.
They turn and run.
That night
the surrealist has horrible nightmares
of the face of the beaver.
The beaver sleeps pretty well.

The Work Force

I was thinking of what
I was going to say
to the workman
who said he'd be here
around 8, how
to explain how writing
is the thing *I* do,
the way he saws and hammers,
but now it's after 9
and he's still not here,
except in this poem.

High Whoosh

When the crowd of Chinese girls
clamored for my autograph
I gave it happily, stunned,
in a calligraphic script
as if I were writing in Chinese
on a long scroll that called for
a long unrolling of my name,
ending with a fluid whoosh across the sky
and up I went
into the stars!

The Field

Every once in a while white
lines appear in my field
of vision, curling sometimes
at the top of it and I
realize once again that there
is an invisible rectangle
around everything.
How do I know it's there?
I just put it there,
that's how.
And those white lines?
Little hairs
straggling from my eyebrows.

A Rowboat of Happiness

Every time I see the expression *mutatis mutandis*
I get grumpy
because
1) It looks and sounds ugly.
2) I can never remember what it means.
3) That makes me feel less intelligent than I like to think I am.
4) It's often used by people who want to sound more intelligent
    than they are
and now a full blast
of sunlight hits the wet grass.

It's Nice

to end on a spot
marked X
knowing that Y and Z
don't matter:
Y has become clouds
and Z the sky above,
blue and white, lovely.

Telegram

This morning about 4
I was lying in bed thinking
about how I'd be here
in this cabin scribbling away
and how the lines go
as far as the words make them go.

Finally I got up
and went down and made oatmeal,
toast and tea, jasmine,
to put a little bit of China into me
and wake me up, like
a real human who
does whatever he has to do.
Like stop.

In memory of
John Ashbery
Bill Berkson
Tom Clark
Bill Corbett
Bertrand Dorny
Larry Fagin
Ted Greenwald
Tom Raworth

LITERATURE
is not the same thing as
PUBLISHING

Coffee House Press began as a small letterpress operation in 1972 and has grown into an internationally renowned non-profit publisher of literary fiction, essay, poetry, and other work that doesn't fit neatly into genre categories.

Coffee House is both a publisher and an arts organization. Through our *Books in Action* program and publications, we've become interdisciplinary collaborators and incubators for new work and audience experiences. Our vision for the future is one where a publisher is a catalyst and connector.

Funder Acknowledgments

Coffee House Press is an internationally renowned independent book publisher and arts organization based in Minneapolis, MN; through its literary publications and *Books in Action* program, Coffee House acts as a catalyst and connector—between authors and readers, ideas and resources, creativity and community, inspiration and action.

Coffee House Press books are made possible through the generous support of grants and donations from corporations, state and federal grant programs, family foundations, and the many individuals who believe in the transformational power of literature. This activity is made possible by the voters of Minnesota through a Minnesota State Arts Board Operating Support grant, thanks to the legislative appropriation from the Arts and Cultural Heritage Fund. Coffee House also receives major operating support from the Amazon Literary Partnership, the Jerome Foundation, McKnight Foundation, Target Foundation, and the National Endowment for the Arts (NEA). To find out more about how NEA grants impact individuals and communities, visit www.arts.gov.

Coffee House Press receives additional support from the Elmer L. & Eleanor J. Andersen Foundation; the David & Mary Anderson Family Foundation; Bookmobile; Fredrikson & Byron, P.A.; Dorsey & Whitney LLP; the Fringe Foundation; the Kenneth Koch Literary Estate; the Knight Foundation; the Matching Grant Program Fund of the Minneapolis Foundation; Mr. Pancks' Fund in memory of Graham Kimpton; the Schwab Charitable Fund; Schwegman, Lundberg & Woessner, P.A.; the Silicon Valley Community Foundation; and the U.S. Bank Foundation.

The Publisher's Circle of Coffee House Press

Publisher's Circle members make significant contributions to Coffee House Press's annual giving campaign. Understanding that a strong financial base is necessary for the press to meet the challenges and opportunities that arise each year, this group plays a crucial part in the success of Coffee House's mission.

Recent Publisher's Circle members include many anonymous donors, Suzanne Allen, Patricia A. Beithon, the E. Thomas Binger & Rebecca Rand Fund of the Minneapolis Foundation, Andrew Brantingham, Robert & Gail Buuck, Dave & Kelli Cloutier, Louise Copeland, Jane Dalrymple-Hollo & Stephen Parlato, Mary Ebert & Paul Stembler, Kaywin Feldman & Jim Lutz, Chris Fischbach & Katie Dublinski, Sally French, Jocelyn Hale & Glenn Miller, the Rehael Fund-Roger Hale/Nor Hall of the Minneapolis Foundation, Randy Hartten & Ron Lotz, Dylan Hicks & Nina Hale, William Hardacker, Randall Heath, Jeffrey Hom, Carl & Heidi Horsch, the Amy L. Hubbard & Geoffrey J. Kehoe Fund, Kenneth & Susan Kahn, Stephen & Isabel Keating, Julia Klein, the Kenneth Koch Literary Estate, Cinda Kornblum, Jennifer Kwon Dobbs & Stefan Liess, the Lambert Family Foundation, the Lenfestey Family Foundation, Joy Linsday Crow, Sarah Lutman & Rob Rudolph, the Carol & Aaron Mack Charitable Fund of the Minneapolis Foundation, George & Olga Mack, Joshua Mack & Ron Warren, Gillian McCain, Malcolm S. McDermid & Katie Windle, Mary & Malcolm McDermid, Sjur Midness & Briar Andresen, Maureen Millea Smith & Daniel Smith, Peter Nelson & Jennifer Swenson, Enrique & Jennifer Olivarez, Alan Polsky, Marc Porter & James Hennessy, Robin Preble, Alexis Scott, Ruth Stricker Dayton, Jeffrey Sugerman & Sarah Schultz, Nan G. & Stephen C. Swid, Kenneth Thorp in memory of Allan Kornblum & Rochelle Ratner, Patricia Tilton, Joanne Von Blon, Stu Wilson & Melissa Barker, Warren D. Woessner & Iris C. Freeman, and Margaret Wurtele.

For more information about the Publisher's Circle and other ways to support Coffee House Press books, authors, and activities, please visit www.coffeehousepress.org/pages/support or contact us at info@coffeehousepress.org.

Big Cabin was designed by
Bookmobile Design & Digital Publisher Services.
Text is set in New Baskerville.